The Doll with Two Backs

and other poems

MAURICE HARMON

The Doll with Two Backs

and other poems

salmonpoetry

Published in 2004 by
Salmon Publishing Ltd.,
Cliffs of Moher, County Clare, Ireland
Website: www.salmonpoetry.com
email: info@salmonpoetry.com

ISBN 1 903392 45 4

Cover artwork: Great Basin petroglyphs (from Luther Cressman, *Petroglyphs of
Oregon*). Reproduced by courtesy of University of Oregon Books
Cover design & typesetting: Siobhán Hutson

Salmon Publishing gratefully acknowledges the
support of The Arts Council / An Chomhairle Ealaíon

for Susanna

Acknowledgments

Acknowledgement is due to the following publications where some of these poems previously appeared:

Agenda, Cork Literary Review, Cyphers, Journal of Irish Studies, Limestone, Poetry Ireland Review, The Recorder, Ríocht na Midhe, The SHOp.

'Feathers Above the Weir', 'Beside the Griboedov' and 'The North Road' appeared in *Tales of Death and other poems* (2001).

My thanks to the Achill Heinrich Böll Committee for allowing me to stay at the Heinrich Böll cottage where some of these poems were written.

Salmon Publishing and Maurice Harmon wish to thank the John Deaver Drinko Academy of Marshall University and its Director, Dr. Alan B. Gould, for their support of this publication.

In Autumn, 1992, Maurice Harmon occupied the John Deaver and Elizabeth Gibson Drinko Distinguished Chair in Liberal Arts at Marshall University, Huntington, West Virginia. He returned in April 1994 to participate in the John Deaver Drinko Academy Symposium on the "Globalization of Higher Education", and that May he was awarded an Honorary Doctorate of Humane Letters at Marshall University's 157th Commencement.

Contents

"In the spiritual life of the Pueblo Indians of the Southwest, the *kachina* plays a significant role. Whites would call the kachina a 'doll,' but this is only the tangible representation of a spiritual being or 'god' that objectifies particular truths or dynamics of life. The Zuñis of western New Mexico have a kachina heavy with meaning for understanding the history of the Indian frontier. This kachina came out of the underworld fastened back to back with a person from an alien world. The deformity condemned the two to an eternity of physical union in which neither could ever see or understand the other."

(Robert M. Utley. *The Indian Frontier of the American West 1846-1890*)

"...men who could not so much as conceive that behind the outer ring of port-towns, behind those dark Irish bogs with their gleaming pools of water, there was another mode of life as valid, as honourable, as cultured, as complex as their own. They saw nothing there but 'savages,' 'wild hares,' 'beasts,' 'vermin,' 'churles,' 'rascals,' 'felons,' 'slaves,' either to be 'rooted out' and 'civilised' or 'exterminated.'"

(Seán O Faoláin, *The Great O'Neill. A Biography of Hugh O'Neill. Earl of Tyrone, 1550-1616*)

"His nurse had taught him Irish and shaped his rude imagination by the broken lights of Irish myth. He stood towards the myth upon which no individual mind had ever drawn out a line of beauty and to its unwieldy tales that divided against themselves as they moved down the cycles in the same attitude as towards the Roman catholic religion, the attitude of a dulwitted loyal serf."

(James Joyce. *A Portrait of the Artist as a Young Man*)

PART ONE

The Doll with Two Backs

I. Prelude

As the man who has narratives fed
the rope of arrows beyond the crater's rim
and gently let it slide through air and water
the tiny worm folded back upon itself
wet and glistening.

In the beginning, he said, the word
gave origin to the Father
who touched an illusion
who attached the illusion
to a thread of dream.

*

Black were our fathers,
the late born of creation,
cold their skins and scaly
goggled their eyes
membranous their ears
webbed their feet
they crouched when they walked
crawling like toads, newts and lizards
when they first looked full on one another
hid behind skirts of rush and bark
in horror of their filthier parts.

*

What is it that always was
had no beginning
has no ending?

Where is it
that all things have equal value
equal status, equal outcome?

'I speak to the wind
I sing to the tree
I cry in the river'.

*

Despite the bronze cannon and the hot-shot guns
ill-equipped to shape events, lacking tongues
Jefferson's pioneers thought they knew better
gathered facts for the good of all, but sought trade
made fools of those they would make accessories
put a gun to their heads and pleaded, 'Be our
friends'.
Despite the measuring chain and circumferentor
it did not sink beneath their scalps that chiefs
resented being powwowed down to, spat
at medals and cocked hats, scorned those
who sold guns yet urged them not to kill
and did not twig the songs warriors sang.

*

Like you we have grown out of this land.
We are one family, brothers on this land.

The Great Spirit has made us both strong
not to hurt one another, but to assist.
No wrong will ever be done to you by the white man.

*

They saw the strangers hungry
and gave them to eat.

They saw them cold
and gave them fuel.

They saw them horseless
and gave them mounts.

They saw them lost
and gave them guides.

*

When the Army of the West came to Bent's Fort
Yellow Wolf did not need eye-glasses to see behind
tents and campfires stretched like stars along the Arkansas
seventeen hundred men with guns, whitetops ranked and
    set to roll
twenty thousand horses, mules and oxen filling their mouths
General Kearny manifestly destined to crack the whip
Mexico under his satchel, Texas, the Southeast and California
already bagged, Oregon bonded, and when gold shone
in the eye of a millrace, the world and his wife
scourged the plains, white man's weal, writ and water
came down hard from Plymouth Rock to Tillamook.

*

We will give you money, you will not be poor.
You will be just like Americans.
You will be given twenty acres each
yours as long as you stay.
For five years you will be given everything—
cattle, horses, wagons, blankets, hats, coats, flour, coffee.
We will watch over you, build you houses
plough your land, fence it.
The hammer man will mend your wagons
repair your earthbreaker.
The great headman will pay.
You will be just like Americans.

*

The earth is part of my body.
I belong to the land
out of which I came.
The earth is my mother.

You want me to break the land.
Shall I take a knife and tear her breasts?

17

You want me to dig for stone.
Shall I go under her skin and take her bones?

You want me to cut grass and make hay.
How dare I hack my mother's hair?

*

The man who has narratives
created these stories
that we might listen to them
here upon the earth

*

South Wind said, 'I will wear my headband
when I run on trees. I will travel only on limbs'.
When he walked on them boughs broke and fell.

Or he would say, 'Now I will wear this headband
with which I snap off the heads of trees'.

He wore yet another when he levelled trees
as though they had been chopped at the butt.

Rarely he said, 'This time I will wear the headband
with which I suck trees up by the roots'.

But he could not catch the beautiful girl at ocean's side.
Just as he almost touched her, she would disappear.

He thought about her, dreamt of her, saw her often
but did not know what kind of girl she was.
Blue Jay said, 'If you want to catch her, do not blink.
Stare straight at her until you catch her hand.
She is Ocean's daughter from the place beneath the wave
home of the ever-young where nothing withers or fades'.
South Wind did as he was told and caught her hand.
He took her home, he took her south. She did not like it.

He took her back. Her father had everything.
Bull-shouldered whales surged through the depths
seals barked and cried as in the Oregon caves
dolphins soared into the light, porpoises played
beautiful creatures with see-through skins
with luminous eyes, with pulsing gills
all lovely—the slow-moving crabs, loggerheads and
        green turtles
shoals seething forward, then swerving away—
a magical world—flashing, twinkling, spinning, curving
in a boundless melody of sounds and shapes, in
        undiminished plenitude
more beauty than South Wind had ever imagined.

He spoke to Ocean, 'We will be partners from now on.
I will destroy things, you will possess them.
When I wear my headband you will be angry
and drift things and drown things. We will work
        together forever'.

Again he took the daughter to the upperworld
her spine pressing on his, fusing, thickening.

*

Coyote had no wife.
No matter what he did no one wanted him.
Women didn't trust him.
One day as he went to the coast to buy dried salmon
he met two frog-women digging for camas.
    'Where are you going?' they asked.
He pretended not to hear.
When they yelled a third time, he seemed to hear.
    'What do you want?' he asked.
    'Nothing. We've just been trying to ask a question'.
    'What is it?'
    'Where are you going?'

'To the coast, to look for salmon'.
'Will you leave us some on your way back?'
'I will'.
He went on, but thought how he might trick them.
He hadn't gone far when he saw wasps on a branch.
He went to the nest, took it down, and closed it.
Then he put it in his basket.
He put the basket on like a pack, went back to the women,
but did not seem to heed them.

'Hey', they shouted, 'are you going home?'
'Yes, I am'.
'How much salmon do you have?'
'Not very much'.
'You promised to leave us some'.
'Alright, come and get it'.
When they came up he began to untie his pack.

'Look inside', he said.
They did and when they did, he gave his pack a great whack.
The wasps went mad and stung the women to death.
Coyote removed their vulvas.
Now whenever he felt the urge
he would dig a hole in the ground
put those vulvas in, and do it.
Not long afterwards the two women came back to life.
One of them looked and said, 'My vulva's gone! How about you?'
The other looked and said, 'Mine, too!'
They knew who had played this trick on them.
Ever since frogs have no female organs.

*

Coyote tried to drown himself. He did not die.
He built a fire and jumped in. He did not burn, he did not die.

He took a rope and wound it round his neck.
He hauled himself up, but did not die.

He took a knife and cut his throat, but did not die.
He tried in many ways to kill himself, but gave it up.

He cried and cried, but after a while, gave that up.

*

Still with us
He is everywhere
watching all his people
all the creatures He has made
all good and all life
creator, guardian, teacher
we are all here because of Him.

*

Feeding alone, apart from the herd, the old
bull moves massively above the plains
while a man crawls through the long grass.

The buffalo stares at the spot, grazes again, but abruptly
attacks. Stops short. The gunman aims
at the thin shield of bone above the nose.

Sights the chest matted with coarse hair
thick horns blunted and split to the skull
nose and forehead marred with white scars.

They watch and wait under the hot sun.
The man thinks, my friend, if you'll let me off
I'll let you off. The animal turns.

Little by little the width of his side appears.
The gun explodes. The old bull spins
about like a top, gallops away, drops.

White men spit words out like tobacco stains—
'beasts', 'vermin', 'savages', 'filthy in their diet'.

The hero of Atlanta whistles an old refrain—
'Exterminate, exterminate'.

Anatomies of death crawl forth again
a 'salvage nation'.

Old names stride from the mound—
Kearny, Carleton, Connor—
as ready to kill as those at Smerwick and Rathlin.

*

The old chief said, 'I love the prairie.
I wish you would not insist
on putting us on a reservation'.

Kit Carson had the answer:
get them out,
reconstruct,
civilise.

*

Chief Joseph spoke for the Nez Perces.

'I have heard talk and talk
but nothing is done.

Good words do not last long
unless they amount to something.
Words do not pay for my dead people
nor for my country overrun by white men.

They do not protect my father's grave.
I am tired of talk that comes to nothing.

When my father died
his hands were not stained
by the blood of a white man'.

*

They made their marks

Satank, Satanta, Kicking Bird for the Kiowas
Ten Bears, Horse Back, Iron Mountain for the Comanches
Poor Bear for the Kiowa-Apaches
Little Raven for the Arapahos
Black Kettle, Tall Bull, Little Robe for the Cheyenne
Bull Bear pressing so hard he almost lost the head

*

A warrior sang.
'I am the leaves of the tree.
I am the drops of the spring rain.

I have come from what I know not
and there I shall return'.

Although they knew they must
the Nez Perces could not bring themselves to stir
but smoked and talked
in the soothing air
in land given into their care.

The tipis stood
the camp fires burned
meadows, apple blossom and camas flowers
seasoned the wind.

The young chief
placed fresh horseskin and striped poles
above his father's grave.

Who would make the first move?
Who would lead them away?
Who would obey Irish recruits?
Land of shooting waters
place of bitter roots.

*

In the Moon of the Popping Trees
the dead encounter the dead.
Under the great hill old wounds
ooze in the poultice of straw.
When the beast lies down with the man
they turn to dream, ghost shirts
ball dearg.

*

A tree will go green
Our people come together
We will see our dead
We will dance
The earth will shiver
I will make a wind blow
We will see our dead
When the soldiers come about you
Do not be afraid
We will see our dead
In the holy shirts
Sing the song I have taught you
They will drop down dead
They will run
Their horses will sink
The riders will jump

They too will sink
You can cut them down
They will die
All that race will die
My friends, this is straight
This is true

*

Emerging from his brush lodge slowly
he revolved his palms outward to show
the scars inflicted in the old time
when whitemen nailed him to the cross
he preached what they had come to hear—
a land where they would be free
buffalo, elk, pronghorn on vast plains
rivers filling with fish, fields of camas
no sickness, no hunger, no strife—
they abandoned cabins, erected tipis again
performed the ghost dance
chanting, stamping, quickening
some who collapsed returned
to babble what they had seen—
the promised land, no white men
peace, everlasting peace, the old life.

II. Broken Lights, Broken Lances

i

Pushing tea things aside he stretches
the old school map across the table
where, explorers again, they begin
finger-trekking over known places—
Springfield, Worcester, Medford, Lowell, Salem—
only to discover where his has halted, beyond
cups, saucers, jug and sugar bowl
across the dark stains of seeping rivers
across the tomahawk of the mountain chain.
Together, in silence, they read sign language.

On Northwest Orient he knows nobody, feels
no ties, savours the hard vowels of the hostess
the nasal crackle of the Captain's voice
as they drive westward through heedless skies
gaze down from 30,000 feet:
indifferent flat fields, grain towers
machines like caterpillars tracking the earth.
Portland's orange lights come up in bloom.
No one meets him. He walks out to the bus
braced by a white gleam on a remote peak.

He has crossed the Oregon Trail, untried
his shoulder not impressed to any wheel.

*

The spirit that brought them
over the great divide
stiffened Morgan Odell's Old Testament jaw.

God's breath blew through the trees
cooling the lawns
gentling minds and hearts.

In the college's Wayside Chapel
John Anderson, biblical scholar
called the Lord's blessing on their work.

'When thou passes through the waters
I will be with thee
and through the rivers
they shall not overflow thee.

When thou walkest through the fire
thou shall not be burnt
nor shall the flame kindle upon thee'.

*

He looked out of place in the Harris tweed
leather patches stitched to elbows and cuffs
his scuffed initialled briefcase intimating
bow ties, sherry parties, plus fours
his voice, formal and accented, evoking
a distant world. Eager, inexperienced.

*

Dusenbery advised seniors to take the seminar.
'It will do you good', he told them, 'this man
'is like a preacher crossing the plains bringing
gifts of knowledge and soul, raising values'
but the grades he gave, the typed remarks
made them fly to the Head, flapping fingers
rustling papers, babbling complaints, hissing
'Expects East Coast standards from West Coast students'.

Rubbing the worn icon of the white whale
presented recently in silent mockery
Dusenbery refused to interfere.
Unsettled, they took refuge in the cafeteria
and the comfort of coffee, handed essays back

and forth, read the stranger's comments, aghast.
Words like 'rubbish', 'makes no sense', 'prove'
darkened the margins like arrow-heads.

*

Chaucer's freshness quickened his step
the mix and match of teller and tale
narrative man turned out in chequered styles
on a road rising from pub to spire
'Thanne longen folk to goon on pilgrimages'

The Renaissance spirit in sequence and sonnet
became his mood, books of etiquette, memoirs
Raleigh's thoughts on Roanoke
fish, flesh and fowl
'the new found land'

Beginning as they went on
with hype, hassle and ill-judged favours
natural inhabitants posed on plinths
Manteo, Lord of Roanoke and Dasamongueponke
'a most faithfull Englishman'
John White's faithful shapes and fair narratives
betrayal, on both sides, ill-matched
afoul in the land of plenty
the dead like dolls in the charnel house
'flesh clene taken'

*

Even freshman composition fired him up.
Since the codes made sense
he practiced them with a convert's zeal,
saw them like stones set in a pattern
down the dark grain of a planed face.

She had not liked him when she heard him
defining principles of composition
talking of making it new, workable myth.

His picture of writers panning for gold
had no place for those whose rock-faced signs
remained unriddled, features left unclaimed.

*

He sought an ideal, made the term essay
the ultimate prize, as though it were an emblem
they might wear, sign of their coming of age.

The poem on the page a sacred text to him
its meanings not imposed but traced, inferred
from close inspection, clues disclosed—
touch-tone, texture, the tracery of signs.

He loved the entering
the feel of an inner shape when elements fused
the leap of faith where the imagination's
secret flame cleared the lines.

*

Hearing music farther up the hill
he laid aside the blank page
and traced the sound to a tree-house.

Inside in dark outline a figure breathing
plaintive notes, a thin strain
issuing through the skin of green.

The shape self-absorbed
playing directly into the tree
As though the wood exhaled sound

tree and girl in such accord
the spirit lived within the bone.

Disliking auditors
he had not let her sit in
on his Renaissance class.
Enraged, she strode away
mouthing 'British' smugness.

*

Sometimes he tried to imagine how they saw him,
this generation in from the valleys, logging towns
and the coast, on the way back, seeing in him perhaps
an image from far away before hatred or hunger
made them take their chances in the new land.

He was conscious of being different
in voice, manner, shaping
ways of thinking, hardly noticed
little things, a turn of speech
the seals of instinct.

*

He came upon her in a Clackamas pool.
She surged up, sleek as a seal
thrashed across, clambered out, clawed
her way by sapling and tuft, then raced hard
frisky and luminous, along the cliff.

Where others dove, jumped, flung outward
she wrapped her legs close, launched, struck
with a splash, at one with water, lithe as an eel.
It poured from her shoulders, her face intent, her arms
like twin blades, foamed about her like milk.

Watching through a mask of leaves
he yearned to take part, to strip and plunge
into the ancient stream, to salmon-leap
revel in motion, be one with fluidity
enjoy honeyed air on skin and bone.

But kept his place, surprised by this
changeling risen from the abiding deep
that one nervous and withdrawn could be
so unselfconscious here, so elemental
at risk with each bright stroke, striking water.

*

From the Adams cottage in Letterfrack
he had carried a sod of turf
redolent of thatch and byre
Great Plains, lost holdings
songs saved in a book.

Now it brightened the hearth
as strewn on settee and chairs
the Sacagaweans began to sing and sway—
water like wine, this land, overcome—
while the sod spent its medicinal tang.

Apart, her hands stretched to the peat
shaped by those who had dug
in the camas prairies, pulled
soaked, hulled acorns in the oak-groves
steam-cooked fish in the shallow pits

unrolled the feast-mats for potlach
no longer in awe of candlefish
no longer secure in the sea's trace—
'when the tide goes out the table is set'—
no longer attuned to salmon runs.

*

The Salmon-people assumed fish skins
made the run, spawned, then bared their bones
silvery wraiths melting in mud
retracing their way underwave
where they feasted and danced
unless someone mislaid a bone.

*

He read of those who traded with pioneers
worked for them, mated with them, married
but had become dream threads as though
they had never walked and talked in this air.
Wraiths. Absences no one talked about.
The blood-line thinning out beyond recall.

*

Beyond the wood where two rivers joined
when their guts cringed from salmon and camas roots
the pioneers bought all the dogs they could find,
assayed the rapids, discovered great falls—
Horsetail, Latourell, Wahkeena, Multnomah—
spilling through God's hands upon their passage.

'Ocian in view! O! the joy!' At journey's
end Cape Disappointment
an old Baud, ribbons, a bad exchange
frail links with kin and courtly muses.

*

From his upstairs window he would see her
stepping behind the sunflowers on her way
to visit him, hurrying in with a record
Gershwin's 'Rhapsody in Blue'
Debussy's 'Prélude á l'après-midi d'un faune'

Eager as he had been
blotting paper mind
taking in everything that touched it

*

Ordinary as a leaf slipping free
quiet as a chipmunk nibbling in tiny fists
while he raked old brush and leaves

the blackness of her eyes
as she hunkered below
the elevation of sparks

blue smoke
descending like incense
into their lungs

*

As he talked in class he watched to see
if she sensed the handling of line and rhythm
in 'Home-Thoughts from Abroad'
the exactness in bole, leaf, bird, response
flowing like warm breath from line to line
or caught belief's paradigm in 'The Scholar Gypsy'.
'Then fly our greetings, fly our speech and smiles!'

*

Stafford's voice on the phone: 'Kenny, Dusenbery
and I are planning go see *The Oxbow Incident*.
We thought you might want to mosey along'.

Kansas sounds, relaxed, drawn-out
an offhand, cool, appraising tone he aims
to follow in a slow offbeat response.

Across the parking lot in plaid shirts
and jeans they amble forward and apart
with an oblique and wary friendliness.

Colleagues, sons of those who made the long trek
strange placenames in the gullies of their speech
Umatilla, Klamath Falls, The Dalles.

Behind their casual tack and circumspection
forefathers shifted wagons down ravines,
hacked, traded, talking Bible talk.

The Oxbow Incident or *Gun-Fight at the OK Corral*
give scale and style to codes and curbs
reflected still in what they say and are.

*

He read the poem slowly, for its music and rhythm
its line of beauty made and then remade
and in the silence heard a student complain
'I always have trouble with this guy Agamemnon'.

*

Fires in the bark lodges, broken lights.
Once upon a time a chief's daughter
had the death sickness, women marched
around the bed chanting the death song.

A white deer came from the dark forest.
Unafraid, it walked across the grass.
It walked around the tipi three times
and three times looked in at the dying girl.

The third time the white deer came in.
The girl stretched out her hand to it.
The deer came close, kissed her lips
walked into the dark and she was cured.

*

Memaloose that men and women passed in dread
Spirit Lake whose demon dragged them down
the gut at Short Narrows boiling and whirling.

Beyond the campfire within receding depths
of red cedar, maple, black cottonwood—
hunting grounds, sacred trees
the Nez Perces, Shoshoni, Chinook.

*

It was her idea to go camping at Yachats.
Sometimes they hiked back to coyote hill
or explored shoals and creeks along the coast.
The woods were dense, tangled, over-grown
with fresh growth—fern, holly, spruce—
sprouting from mouldering limbs and trunks
melting stumps scaled by lichen, ivy, moss.

The sway of systems undisturbed
of life growing, failing, self-renewed
by what it died into and fed upon.
'Like civilisation', she said, 'if left natural'.

*

Discovering driftwood wedged
beneath a log she pried it loose
then exclaimed, 'It's the doll. It looks
in both directions, the faces never meet.
Neither can ever see or understand the other'.

Taking it from her he looked as she directed
and saw two shapes back to back, two heads
stumps that could be arms, frayed ends
that might be legs, a blind togetherness.

*

He found her crouched beside a pool
absorbed by something held between her hands.
'Look', she cried, placing a dark wafer
onto his palm, 'an arrow-head. From my family'.

The image formed within his mind:
a slender sculpted figure leaning forward
tender flesh curved above her heels
a taut bow-line tensed across her back.

*

Yachats brought them together, lugging things
from the car, sitting about the fire, disclosing
a common story, but even as logs crackled
and sparks soared there were depths beyond them.

Even as they retrieved the past, pulling the cart
of history, the stacked decay pressed downward
the past fumed into their faces.

Gruesome remains turned up
those in the Long Walk, on the Trail of Tears
who trudged to Hell or Connacht.

The bull that tore at *Carraic-an-phuill*
pawed the ice at Bear River.
What rid the land of lord and chief
put paid to Modoc and Chinook.

*

Sidney bestrode the south
burning, butchering.

Gilbert, knighted in the field
did nothing by halves.

If he took a castle
slaughtered them all.

All Renaissance men—
Sidney, Gilbert, Perrot
Carew, Spenser, Barnabe Rich—
limbering up for Roanoke.

*

Colin Clout averted his gaze
when O'Brien's foster mother
sucked blood and smeared it
over face, breasts and hair.

*

Once she scratched upon the ground
scoring, digging, jabbing. The stick
she used shaped whitetops, iron horses, talking wires
grubbers, grabbers, panners, pedlars.

The more she talked the more it raced
until her words dragged behind its fierce intent.

Names fell from her, generals, agents, chiefs.
Fierce and dangerous, she strode above him
as though it was he had left her in State care
as though on him she could scratch and tear.

ii

Things she said

long ago when the mountains were people
when the Sky Spirit came down to earth
he put his finger to the ground

wherever he touched
a tree grew
wherever he walked
snow melted
rivers ran

Grey Wolf burnt everything in the old world.
Then talked with the Sun.
'There should be a flood', he said.

When it came a woman and a dog
fled to the top of Tacobud and hid there
from them were born the next race of people

*

Little things

Watching her trace
trickles of moisture
on the window-pane with a finger-tip

Absorbed

Seeing her brooding and remote
he knew the pity from his bones

A hundred years ago
wars, treaties, reservations
howitzers, long-range rifles
the mighty hangman

Janus-faced, rifle in one hand
peace-pipe in the other
smoke either way

Seeing what loosenings and diminishments
what fadings and runnings-out
tribes drained from the basin
gone to ground
coastal families dissolved in mist

*

His study in disarray,
papers and notes here and there on a long table,
memos between his chair and the door.

She put the dictionary, thesaurus
and reference works within reach,
noted signs of the poem he was writing
a framed quotation upside down

'One day together, for pastime, we read
   Of Launcelot, and how Love held him
      in thrall'.

*

Alert as a blue jay
when he read her a draft of the poem

Odds and ends put together

How could he recover lost threads
that linked her and hers to him and his

The common story
Desmond in rags
O'Neill harried and humbled
The Queen far off in her counting-house

*

He read what she wrote after his class.

'You talk about analogies
the beginning of civilisations
pagan, christian. I see
proximity, not communion.
The indifferent beak lets her drop.
That means failure, disappointment,
betrayal, when a powerful figure
abandons the weaker'.

*

Her head above him shifted and wavered
like an image in stirred water, the barbs
of her breasts lunged against his face.

The heat from her body surged through him,
her thighs' suck a rip tide
tearing away flesh and blood.

When she was done she reared back
with three great thrusts of her wings
leaving him empty as a crock

From which the last of the bleached eggs
has been taken, the worm folded
back upon itself, milksop.

He told her the story of Bébhionn.
who was beautiful but exceedingly tall.
Knowing she was not of their time
the Fian were awed and terrified.
She had a diadem of gold,
a crimson cloak with a golden brooch.
They asked her to lean against the hill
so that they might converse with her.
She told them she came from The Land of Women
and had been given in marriage to a man from
    The Land of Men.

'I was given to him three times and three times I escaped.
This is the third time. I have come to you for protection'.
She placed her hand in Goll's hand.
He was a wave of death over fierce bands.
She had three golden rings on one hand
two on the other, each as wide as a man's arm.
When she removed her helmet
her hair fell about her in eight score shining tresses.

When they gave her a goblet of water
she poured the water into her right hand
drank three sips, raised her hand
and sprinkled the rest over the gathering.
Everyone laughed.
Fionn asked, 'Why did you not drink from the goblet?'
'In all my life', she replied, 'I have never drunk
from a vessel that did not have a rim of silver or gold'.

They saw an even bigger man approaching.
He wore a green cloak with a brooch of gold.
He had a branchy shield red as a rowanberry
a gold-hilted sword in one hand
a blue-angled spear in the other.

They were terrified.

'Who is he?', Fionn asked.

'My husband', Bébhionn replied and sat between
Fionn and Goll.

The man came towards them. He, too, was very beautiful.

No one knew what was in his mind.

He raised his hand and made a wicked cast at Bébhionn.

It went through her and came out her back to the length
of a man's hand.

He pulled the spear to him and went out through
the gathering.

'You saw that', said Fionn. 'Let anyone who will not
avenge the deed
think no more of being in the Fian'.

They followed him towards the harbour.

He went into the sea where four caught up with him.

Caílte cast his spear. It went through the sling
of his shield and into his left shoulder.

The buckler fell. When he used his right hand
to remove the spear, Caílte caught the other spear.

When he tried to cast the waves intervened.

A great ship appeared from the west.

The man went on board and no one knew which
direction it took.

Bébhionn said, 'Prepare my grave, arrange my burial.
I came to you for protection and died in your care'.

*

She saw him hammering a ball
running set-faced to and fro, from side
to side, as though he knew this banging, anticipation
return achieved nothing, yet still he struck
still drove it back to where it rebounded
with a fierce resilience like a trapped bird.

*

At the end of the night
after someone had thrown fresh logs on the fire
and someone had changed the tune
a wizened creature started to dance
releasing her body out of its hoop
raising her arms, moving with power
and when she drew him onto the floor
he responded in kind, not missing a beat
they were stepping with style, in tune with the sound
flexing their bodies, not wanting to stop
and when she beckoned him out of the house
she led by the hand, he was willing to go
she was pulling him down to root and mould
leading him on, he was willing to follow
but when she seized him high and low
he could not give as good as she gave
and found his way back, in loss and shame
where someone had thrown fresh logs on the fire
and someone had changed the tune.

iii

When you see this tree remember
it is a witness we were friends.
Never cut down this tree.
Let the arm be broken that would hurt it.
Let the hand wither that would break a twig of it.
So long as snow shall fall on Mount Hood let it stand.
So long as the white deer shall come from the forest let it stand.
Let children play around it.
Let boys and girls dance under its boughs.
Let old men smoke together in its shade.
Let old women know contentment in its roots.
Let this tree be for all time.

*

Drawn by talk of partnership
he went to watch.

The quarterback could find his mate
racing sometimes to the right
sometimes to the left
now fast, now slow, now in a sudden burst
or speeding upfield ready to turn
ball and player meeting as though by secret call.

Even when opposing players tried to keep him checked
to stay his course, he could be elusive as a leveret
      pursued by hounds
doubling back, hiding, only to arise in that bright
      moment to collect the pass
the hard shot to the chest, the high lob, the bullet fired
      to the end zone
the bond between them so instinctive

it was like water flowing
the moving, unpredictable figure, now visible
now racing where least expected
the thrower waiting, protected
given time, moving back, watching
waiting for the silken shape to meet his eye.

Attuned as eagles rising from the earth
cavorting, spinning, lifting on columns of air
one fully grown, the width of her wings wide as
    a grown man
he, agile and alert, aware of every feint
and turn, her compact pivots
and wheels
while he held his ground
the steady consort for her gyres and spiralings.

*

It was a silence no one heard
no one talked about
a stillness that lingered

an absence in which what had been
was no longer felt
a loss no one was reckoning

in the faces of those he met
in the voices, the memories
the mementos in house and barn

nothing he could put his hand on
nothing anyone could show him

saying this belonged to those who used to be
this implement, this bit of cloth, this worn moccasin
this pony, this remnant of a headdress

the landscape held its secrets
under the great pines
behind the falls, along the swift rivers

in the lichen and the water weed
an impenetrable stillness

*

Before the year ended
before she handed in her final paper
before she sat the examinations
without explanation

Like a sudden bereavement
a cold snap in May

The state inert under thick cloud, paths sodden
borders and banks slipping beneath his feet.
He walked where the Tillamook burn showed bare
    and black
where deer had starved at racks of fallen trees.

Dull and receding water gleamed in the distance
like memory gone blank

'Wo ho ho he cries, awaie she flies,
    and so her leaue she takes.
This wofull man with wearie limmes,
    runnes wandring round about'

PART TWO

The Right Note

In the Year of Our Lord 2004
I tried to turn over a new leaf
with a firm purpose of amendment
but the parchment stuck to my hand.
My soul was not for turning.

I wanted to clear the ground,
to dig down, expose debris,
shake it loose to establish
fresh seeds, amend conditions, but
the soil was stale, its rankness stank.

I seized the axe and cut hard, tried
to get rid of old growth, to disentangle
branches. No matter how hard I worked
fibres held, refusing to snap, their
stringy sinews tenacious as pain.

I can never get free of attachments, nor shake
them off like a dog escaping from water.
Gnarled and weathered, I must knuckle down,
attend to the yield of old limbs,
keep faith with the past, know my place.

Wouldn't it be Great?

'Wouldn't it be great', the not-so-young poet
says to me, 'to write even one poem
that would survive? It's been done, you know'.

Gathered into the everlasting by a single work,
included in anthologies, mentioned in histories,
identified in a footnote: 'remembered for one poem'.

I look at my young friend whose eyes look
out at me beneath a half-dome of frayed hair.
I know how hard he tries, networking, cultivating

editors, turning up reliably at poetry readings
book launches, literary funerals, retentive
of first names as a politician, never missing

an opportunity, and think, Lord, let it be soon.
Let him write one poem editors will quickly realise
makes a significant contribution, at this point in time.

Feathers above the Weir

Last month I could see them feeding,
sparrows, tomtits, blackbirds, the robin.
Flickering against the leaves, performing leaps
and twirls on the outside in full view.

In the pond families of ducks and ducklings
scurrying about, heads steeped in weed and muck,
waterhens no bigger than my thumb
presenting a nib of beak for tiny drops.

Today feathers float above the weir.
Crouched in the reeds mallards in disguise.
Under the rowan a blackbird going brown.
They are shedding, letting go, keeping faith.

Sexless, songless, brooding, torpid, getting
through it. The spirit sags, the system slows.
I know this state—being and non-being—
the hush, the lack of drive, the loss of pith.

The grass slows. Leaves are dog-eared.
No gleam, no shine. I mope above the desk,
sitting it out, this dry patch, soul-sap,
my mind on its own, numbskull, while pages wait.

The Long Haul

I'm here for the long haul, an old dray-horse
has done his rounds. They taught me to walk, taught
me to halt, snaffled spirit, bitted soul.

No more. I've taken a shine to unmarked ways,
forgotten paths, unapproved roads, lanes
I knew before the halter age, rampant

From lack of use, one went to the national school.
I roam about, see life in a frayed branch,
kick up heels, drink from the waters of reverie.

It looks like aimlessness but that's the key.
In time the dunce in the corner misses nothing.
I'm sometimes asked 'how do you put in time?'

I shy away, refuse fences, escape
the stop-watch mind. I've set aside bridle days.
From where I lie it's a clip-clop to eternity.

The Sword

Back again on the old paths I note
the fields curve softly to the trees
and buoyed by the panache of Rockabill
riding high in a vast and constant sea
and the tall ships of the Mournes
coursing firmly through the sky
do not mind so much this time
the pain at the avenue's end
or even the new wall that checks
the blink of sealight through the bars.

Lying on the grass to watch pennants
of white cloud flying out to sea
I remember that last night a sword
studded with gems hung above my head
clear as day and I felt immovable.

Schoolboy

A boy I knew in school
who shared a desk with me for Latin and Greek
lodged in my guilty mind for years
because I failed him.

Every day I watched his pain at the hands of a bully
a toad with a cross stuck through his cincture
like a weapon of righteousness.

Every day, as the boy failed to recite irregular verbs
possessive pronouns
hic haec hoc
hunc hanc hoc
hujus hujus hujus
failed to translate the assigned piece of Caesar or Livy
got his homework wrong, mismatching noun and adjective
used the possessive case when it should have been
　　the accusative
mixed up singular and plural
used a past tense when it should have been the conditional
so confused by fear, pain and humiliation
he was incapable of thought.

Every day Father Murphy dug his thumbnail
into the boy's ear and dragged him along like a dumb beast
or put him kneeling on the boards, his book shaking
while he struck him viciously upon the head.

(What made him think he could force memory to work
the mind to focus, the nerves to settle?
Bitterness he had to live his days teaching
instead of garnering souls in the Far East or the Philippines?
Frustration he should spend his vigour driving adolescents
    like sheep
into the pen of grammar and text
through a field we churned to mire in our clumsiness?)

What has stuck in my mind is the knowledge
I should have gone to the Head. The trouble
the poor excuse I clung to, was that I didn't know better.

I had my quaking heart, my pain when the nail
ran in, when my skull swooned under the white fist.
By staying dumb I backed daily humiliation.

Going Home

a small boy walks behind his mother
walks   half-walks   dream walks
his mind   his entire being   taken
to reverie   dream   or something between

there is no word   for this state
children enter   where they stray
not listening   no longer aware they
have a part in what we are

this   their inner place   we cannot know
although   we too   must have been there
in the long ago   have had that absent air
they bring back nothing from wherever they've been

never mention it merely return
unaware they have been anywhere

Spitting Sticks

i

Avid for tales, I lived with fear, words
were lanterns lifted into the dark, her voice
rose, sank, gasped, quickened, cried.

'Jack! Jack! Come back, come back, don't do it'.
'Oy schmell de blud of an Oirishmon'.
'Oh, Grandmama, what big eyes you have!'

Sent deep into Hampton's woods, the girl strayed
bending for bluebells, daisies, buttercup, singing
as she rounded the gable, skipped into the room.

ii

Fee, fi, fo, fum, blood.
All he could do was run, climb back, down,
down, down, the giant coming fast.

He seized the axe, slashed at the tree, hard.
It swayed, listed, crashed through the rook wood,
buckled the tracks, gouged the sea fields.

Stretched as far as Rockabill, the ocean
hissed and boiled, the thick pelt filled,
the body sank slowly to the rocky floor.

Crabs, lobster, crayfish gorged themselves,
attacked the eyes, ripped into chest and ribs,
gripped and sucked deep at the black heart.

iii

Above my head dark voices whispered
a strange picture of a woman wailing
at the backs, faces anxious, voices taut.

Advancing from the estate foxes were seen
gathered together before the castle, muzzles
raised to the room where the master slept.

Weasels in the hedge bared sharp teeth
The cornered rat turned, faced me down.
The ferret in the burrow filled with blood.

Water won't quench fire, fire
won't burn stick, stick won't
beat dog, we shan't get home tonight.

iv

In Ardgillan a priest lured my brother to the cliffs
with thoughts of vocation, God's work.
His mouth took the boy's breath away.

In Streamstown the Prior's hands, reverent
with paten and host, shared body, blood,
spittle, beast-drool on shining linen.

In Limerick they knew the boy from the woods
would have to be curbed. Observing the set of his jaw
they took out bone. Seeing the look in his eyes

They lowered the lids. Knowing his thoughts
were bent on bird-flight and cloud-dance
they spent years trying to lure him down.

Words

My mind is stuck upon silence like a door
with swollen jambs, my tongue is a lead
weight heavy with disuse. Should we meet

Don't expect me to prattle. I'm fed upon quiet.
The man I knew best kept himself to himself.
Thick as thieves we were quiet as mice.

I'll take your snap a thousand times.
My desk is stuffed with undeveloped smiles.
Unburden. My mind is a dark confessional.

I can listen forever, your secrets are safe.
I never blab. At school had that rapt look
teachers like. They never understood why

I had nothing to say. A connoisseur of word
disorders I can spot an impediment a mile away,
feel for those who beat about the bush or drop

vowels and consonants into a drum. Hum, hum.
Here's my hand. Women, expect no charm.
I like proximity. My heart goes out to you.

An Old Constraint

For several years a neighbour came and went
as though she slipped through the veil
of invisibility, effecting a life I did not follow.

Occasionally I would see her in her garden
tending roses, dead-heading,
or reclined in a deckchair under the apple boughs.

Since she was not in the habit of taking notice
I never stopped. Her cultivated accent
put me off. If we met on the footpath, I might pause

to try a few words, remark on the weather
and in time despite her aloofness came to like her—
her refinement, the warmth when she spoke

of a radio play or a novel, more recently
of an Autumn school in the west she liked to attend.
Even then I could not miss signs

of a slow dissolve that made her shoulder-bones
recede, her face retract like stretched cloth.
The illness grew. I heard she had gone for treatment,

observed the blinds drawn, the car unmoved.
Then she would reappear, paler, reserved, finely
poised. We never referred to what she was going through

and ever since she died I have regretted
the old constraint that weighed upon my tongue,
an impediment we should long since have overcome.

Somebody's Aunt

Some of us you can't take anywhere.
Speechless with pills, slumped in chairs,
droopy as unwatered flowers, or dithering near a door.

Not me. I'm holding on, holding out.
The sap rises, blood burns when a man
Strides through the hall in a flurry of warmth

For some old dear who is hardly able to purse
her lips for a single kiss. He should try me.
Now and then my nephew appears, all smiles

A bunch of grapes or box of chocolates held
in his hand as though they belonged to somebody else.
My niece becomes embarrassed when I take her hand

Inquiring how her father is, does he remember me,
the times we had, the trips, the plans? Silly
questions. Of course he remembers. I do.

Widows proliferate here. We go to seed.
Not me. I'm still invited to weddings.
I fit in. I can be counted on. I know my place.

Just because my face is crumpled as a crushed skirt
My blue rinse curly as baby fern does not mean
I should be hidden away like somebody's aunt.

I'm not somebody's aunt. I'm me, me, me.

Beside the Griboedov

He is no match for her in his black suit,
his starched front, his bottle of champagne.
She floats, pirouettes, moves to unseen strings,
her arms outstretched to imaginary wings.

This is her day, her only day, nothing
will mar the perfection of its play.
She trips to one side, then to the other,
circles the space, uplifted, smiling, free.

Waist-high above the gilded rail,
her white dress shines, her white flowers blaze.
Graceful beside the Griboedov, resplendent
where steeple and dome shimmer and disappear.

She is making the best of it, upholding
the slender glass of her form, beyond
remembering or seeing into the years.
Her bronze boy lifts her high in his arms.

Supporting her, kissing her, wanting to believe.
She responds, knowing she should, but her heart
is in the moment, the little runs, the perfect poses,
arching her body, on her toes, sweeping—left, right.

This is her day, her only day, nothing
will put her off, not love, not the communal flat.
She lifts the hoop of her skirt and glides.
Her steps elegant, her legs like stems of glass.

She is young, she is beautiful, she is keeping
the dream. They will do it right, will soar
above the canal, the spilled blood,
forgetting themselves in speckled depths.

Without Reservation

I am told that the girl in the white dress
who waves after the taxi where the tall man
in uniform sits stiffly upright as he is driven
away and that the girl in the floral dress who walks
to the edge of the lawn and waves after the taxi
where the tall man in dress uniform sits
stiffly upright as he is driven away
do so without reservation.

I do not know why the man in dress uniform
who sits stiffly upright in the black taxi
as he is driven away neither turns his head
to the left where the lady in white stands
like a picture or to the right where the lady
in pink almost blends with the lilac tree
nor makes any attempt to acknowledge their devotion
but stares straight ahead without reservation.

Were I the man in dress uniform who sits
stiffly upright in the taxi as he is driven
away and knows that two beautiful ladies
are waving to him one from the door of the house
where she stands like a picture between the portals
and one from the edge of the lawn beside the lilac
I would want to wave in reply to their devotion
left and right and to do so without reservation.

Retirement

for Tomás Ó Coincheannain

No such thing as retirement.
Doing what you've done for years,
keeping a close eye on the script
to find those tell-tale ends and loops,
as sure as finger-print or trace of DNA.

As able as ever, even more skilled now
to name the scribes whose hands you've found,
to follow the genealogical trail,
to leave your mark in *Éigse* and *Celtica*.

No such thing as easing back.
Engaged, alert, you live with pen in hand
and need no other staff to find your way.

The North Road

One time I knew this road, could tell you
who lived in every house, could tell the smell of each,
could see the gibbet of hats and coats,
the brace of walking sticks,
the poorly-lit passage back to the kitchen,
the chill scullery.
Even if I never entered,
never set foot on the worn flags,
or stepped on the faded lino,
I had it off by heart, what they ate,
their holy pictures—the fly-spotted
Sacred Heart, the opaque red lamp,
the Infant of Prague, the hidden coin,
the Mother of Perpetual Succour
and the dangling shoe.
I could tell what children learnt at school—
tables, spelling, lists, the heart facts.

It was not strange.
It knew its characters, its main events.
The farmhouse fired by a train's spark,
the spot where the driver
aimed the wheel like a gun
and squashed two weasels flat.
Behind that lane old Major Fillgate lived,
frail, stooped, attending his daughters,
courteous in gesture and tone.
Another beauty now: a girl walking
from the old pub, so queenly proud
no one talked to her.
From that dull, two-storey house
another boy set off one day for school
and never came back, knocked down, there.
Hundreds walked in his funeral.

From a labourer's cottage not far from here
Oscar Trainor, pensioner, boarded every Friday,
dragging the heavy sack of his body up the steps,
his sagging flesh straining against his coat.
His famine cottage sinking back to mud,
the thatch black, overgrown, one window boarded up.
On wet days the stench from his clothes filled the bus.
He might have climbed out of the earth.
Gormanstown, Julianstown, Paynestown,
the Black Bull, Delvin, Nanny, Boyne,
the long descent to Cromwell's town,
the gate-towers, the holy spires,
the old river filling between walls my father knew.
The Bull Ring, the Fair Green where
he heard horse traders cracking palms,
beyond these his other world—
high cross, round tower, Cooley, the gap of the north.

The king rode south from here.
I know where his blacksmith lies,
where the headless coachman drove,
where Collier the Robber hid,
where Tone lodged and O'Connell slept,
where the stagecoach stopped.
Man O' War, Balrothery Inn, The Cock.
Behind the pitted surface of this black road
the horse-tamer, the wave-charger,
the old strife, the saint's fire.
I could show you standing stones,
finger marks in rock, a cairn's increase, a pirate's cove,
names straddling a double-ditch—
Bearnagaoire, Ardgillan, Balscaddan, Tubbersool,
Hampton, Fancourt, Bellewstown—
all the one to us, old sounds—'boord',
'jant', 'tay', older words, 'wore', 'dalk'.

The sea a blade held to the throat of the Mournes.
On stormy nights ships hugging the coast
rode the voices of the deep.
Across these waves a woman came to lure
a hero in the old enchantment.
Across these waters animal heads thrust
into rivers and coves, to this cul-de-sac
invaders, adventurers, the disaffected,
the defeated followed the sun's blink.
Across these waters scholars, raiders,
mind seekers—reluctant islanders—
reclaimed courts, cathedrals, schools,
and made their marks.

I could make magic too.
But this is real, the old road part of me,
an artery strafed by rain, the bay
from Skerries to Clogherhead a seething cauldron.
I cycled this road to Streamstown,
the ditches decked with Queen Anne's Lace,
hawthorn's communion cloth,
the chestnut's candelabra,
the rowan's offerings
beech canopies,
grasslands kings desired,
woods ringing with song,
sturdy stands.
My holy road, my pilgrim path, my royal way.

Changed. Obscured. Curves,
groves, hedgerows, habitats
ripped apart.
Defiles of dual carriageway,
chicanes, restraints, controls.
Bungalows, Grecian columns, Spanish arches.

A shrinking hand has reached from Moymel to Mullingar,
deep into Cork and Kerry,
has even clamped west of Shannon,
ring roads, roundabouts, ramps.
Old roads have gone astray.
My North Road has lost its way.

Notes

Any general history of the United States and of Ireland will provide relevant background material for *The Doll with Two Backs*, as will any anthology of Native American literature and legend, but those listed below may be particularly helpful.

Ambrose, Stephen E., *Undaunted Courage. Meriwether Lewis, Thomas Jefferson, and the Opening of the American West* (1996).

Berleth, Richard, *The Twilight Lords. The epic struggle of the last feudal lords of Ireland against the England of Elizabeth I* (1978).

Brown, Mark H., *The Flight of the Nez Perce: A History of the Nez Perce War* (1967).

Feltskog, E.N. (ed.), *Parkman. The Oregon Trail* (1969).

Harmon, Maurice, *The Colloquy of the Old Men* (2001).

Ramsey, Jarold (comp. and ed.), *Coyote Was Going There. Indian Literature of the Oregon Country* (1977).

Sanders, Thomas E., and Walter W. Peek, *Literature of the American Indian* (1973).

Utley, Robert M., *The Indian Frontier of the American West 1846-1890* (1984).